RIDING THE EMOTIONAL ROLLER COASTER

The Emotional Journey of Caring

Sylvia Bryden-Stock

Author's Tranquility Press
ATLANTA, GEORGIA

Copyright © 2024 by Sylvia Bryden-Stock

All rights reserved. No part of this publication may be reproduced, distributed, or transmitted in any form or by any means, including photocopying, recording, or other electronic or mechanical methods, without the prior written permission of the publisher, except in the case of brief quotations embodied in critical reviews and certain other noncommercial uses permitted by copyright law. For permission requests, write to the publisher, addressed "Attention: Permissions Coordinator," at the address below.

Sylvia Bryden-Stock/Author's Tranquility Press
3800 Camp Creek Pkwy SW Bldg. 1400-116 #1255
Atlanta, GA 30331, USA
www.authorstranquilitypress.com

Ordering Information:
Quantity sales. Special discounts are available on quantity purchases by corporations, associations, and others. For details, contact the "Special Sales Department" at the address above.

Riding the Emotional Roller Coaster: The Emotional Journey of Caring/Sylvia Bryden-Stock
Paperback: 978-1-962492-14-0
eBook: 978-1-962492-15-7

DEDICATION

This book is dedicated to my dear husband Brian who has always supported my Life Purpose activities.

In spite of his Young Onset Alzheimer's Disease, he could communicate to me how much he loved me until the end of his journey. This alone proves to me that we must appreciate everything in life and to always—

"LIVE IN THE MOMENT WITH GRATITUDE"

INTRODUCTION

Life is full of challenges that affect our emotions. One could say that through life we are constantly riding a roller coaster of emotional ups and downs.

I don't know of anyone who has not experienced at least one situation during their life that has dramatically challenged the way they handle things.

Things are going well according to our perception of this earthly life until suddenly we are like a pet budgerigar that has fallen off his perch and landed smack bang to the bottom of the cage!

Why is it we think that life should be without any challenges?

Would we not get bored if life was all plain sailing?

What purpose would there be to life if we had no challenges to get through?

Where would our inner strength and tenacity arise from?

Table of Contents

1 And So It Was 1
2 Confusion and Chaos 5
3 You are on your own! 9
4 Alighting the Roller Coaster 13
5 Is There a Stop to this Ride? 16
6 The Secret to Finding the Stop Button 20
7 Letting Go of the Guilt 25
8 Making Denial a Positive Tool 29
9 Dealing with Frustration and Anger 34
10 Getting to Grips with Grief 38
11 Turning Learnings Into Service 42
About the Author 46

1 _And So It Was_

If you had been with me in the January of 2010, you would be witnessing a day that I had known was to come but still had butterflies as big as elephants in my tummy.

Prior to this day I had been discreetly carrying out research into Alzheimer's Disease symptoms to confirm my fears around traits my then partner, now husband, was manifesting. You see, my nursing background and Care Home Management told me that the lovely Brian was most likely on the road to being diagnosed with Young Onset Alzheimer's Disease.

Being someone who is open and honest in her character, it was not easy living a "normal" life with my man, whilst all the while observing the subtle changes that were taking place, probably going unnoticed by people around me.

Then, of course, there is the challenge of finding that moment when one could tenderly confront him with some minor issues he was facing.

Thus began the grievous diagnostic journey of around one year's duration, involving blood tests and numerous scans.

The fateful day dawned in early January of 2010. We went together to see the local Elderly Care and Dementia Consultant at St Peters Hospital in Chertsey for the results following a Specht Scan, MRI scan, X-rays, and Blood tests.

We arrived at the clinic and waited our turn in the clinic. After what seemed a lifetime, a short, kindly looking gentleman with dark hair and eyes that oozed empathy came out of one of the consulting rooms and greeted us "Hello Mr. Stock. Hello Sylvia– come on in and take a seat" It was a typical consulting room layout with desk in front of a large, slightly grubby window and chair behind. Two chairs were placed for us - Brian by the side of the desk facing the consultant and mine so that I could communicate with him if need be. On the desk was a computer with the screen turned away from our view.

Dr Jones leaned forward and in his typically soft caring voice asked Brian how he was. As was usual the immediate response came "I'm fine. I feel really good!" "I'm pleased to hear that" came the response with a smile. Then he began to turn the computer screen a little and I cringed as I began to catch site of the brain image!

"Mr. Stock – I have some good news and some bad news" Although I knew what was coming my palms were sweating and my mouth dry. I looked at my man who I loved so much and watched silently as the communication continued -

"Mr. Stock – the good news is that you have not had any mini strokes, you haven't got any tumors in your brain, neither do you have cancer." Then what I had anticipated, but still did not want to hear, was announced to dear Brian.

Turning the computer screen around so that I had full view he seemed to take a deep breath as if he did not want to give the news – "Mr. Stock, I have to tell you that you have got Young Onset Alzheimer's Disease" I looked at the screen that showed a brain image with what appeared to be around 60% of brain neurons dead!

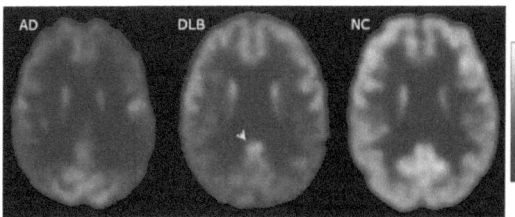

Brian's Brain looked like the one on the right!

Then I hear my man say "Well I feel great! I'm fit and well. I will just have to get on with it."

"Because you are in the younger age onset group, I will prescribe a fairly new drug especially for this called Aricept and you can have the higher dose of 10mgs per day at bedtime." He looks at Brian with deep empathy "I am sorry to have to give this news, but this drug is said to hold it back. I'll see you again in three months to see how you are getting on but before you go, I need to you to do a little test for me."

Then the typical memory scoring test is done and Brian scores 25/30 which means he is very early on in the disease process.

While the test is taking place, I look again at the computer screen and wonder how my lovely man is actually coping as well as he is! Then I realize that he is still capable of doing most things well due to all the past programs and memories that have been laid down in the neurons and operate at an unconscious level.

Homeward bound with Brian understandably in shock, I reassured him that he would have my love and support throughout the journey, that life would continue pretty much as normal, dealing with challenges when they arose.

A much-needed coffee stop was next as we both were coming to terms with what potentially lay ahead.

Many of you reading this book will have your own memories of diagnosis time with Alzheimer's, Dementia, or any other challenging situation with a loved one - including your beloved child.

Any situation where you are thrown into the role of carer will have very similar emotions that manifest along the way. No two people will cope with the carer journey in the same way, but this book is written to highlight key emotions that kick in and their derivative which will not totally be associated with current circumstances.

I can assure you that my nursing and care management background along with Master Coaching skills and a deep spiritual faith did not fully prepare me for the Alzheimer's journey.

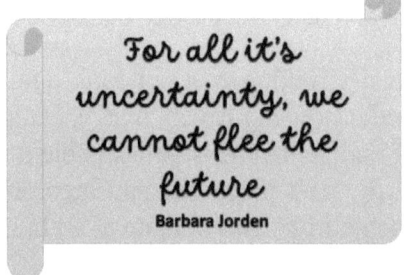

For all it's uncertainty, we cannot flee the future
Barbara Jorden

2 *Confusion and Chaos*

So here it is! The journey begins.

What happens Now? I was blessed with a nursing and care home management background and had already done pre-diagnosis research and had a pretty good idea how to proceed - live as normal and deal with challenges. Somewhere in my head I had it all worked out.

Then thoughts race through your mind about how long before it gets worse. How long has he got?

Any little thing that seems "different" and you think the disease is exacerbating at a phenomenal rate. Conversely you think you imagine it all and tomorrow it will all go away in spite of that inner voice telling you "No, this is it".

Then there is the telling of family members who say, "Well actually we have noticed something for ages and he wouldn't go to the doctor!" What if it was them in the same position, you ask yourself? Would they rush to the doctor shouting "I think I have Alzheimer's Disease" No they would not!

Oh, the initial form filling to claim this and that as advised by the Alzheimer's Society. They are doing their best to help but it is too much to take in. Never mind the fact that the one diagnosed is in complete denial about needing support - "You must come to the Young Onset Group that meets once a week where you will meet others on the journey."

The carer thinks it is a great idea but the one in denial is Definitely not going to go "I want to get on with my life and not have to be reminded all the time when I feel perfectly alright!" A valid response one might say, especially if some are further down the road than you are. It is done with the very best of intentions. Also, it depends if you like playing dominoes and other games or doing some kind of craft and interactive game. Oh my! How are we going to do this journey with someone who has limited interests? Whose key interests have been Folk Singing along with heading up a successful Barn Dance Band for around thirty years.

Grudgingly he attends the monthly coffee and lunch and actually quite enjoys it! There are other carers present as well and some sensible conversations can take place. My particular challenge is the ploughman's lunch when I am wheat and dairy intolerant!! Well, I suppose a few crisps and grapes will keep me going!

You have to somehow find a whole new way of living life as very soon it totally revolves round the person with the condition. However much you love them emotional turmoil seems to kick in as time goes on.

One could say that you now board the ongoing grief train that has no definite journey completion. Who knows how long it will go on for?

Every day you hope for the miracle that will take it all away and life can be "normal again". Even the author had her own chaotic times, despite the background experiences and Master Coaching skills!

You try to keep things as quiet as possible, but word seems to get around somehow and the sympathy pours in - sometimes when life is fairly OK, and you are not thinking about the road ahead. Suddenly you are jolted into the potential future journey once more! How must the one with the diagnosis feel at these times? We will never know apart from them saying that they do not wish to talk about it.

Those who understand the power of empathy rather than sympathy will ask how you are and react accordingly to the patient's upbeat responses along with finding a subtle way to communicate with you, the carer.

Then you find yourself becoming more aware of symptoms emerging and frustrations from the patient causing angry outbursts which maybe have been part of their make-up before. It is all so confusing as moods and behaviour swing from one way to another.

How does one get this unpredictable journey into a manageable pattern?

You don't know how to deal with it and begin to beat yourself up inwardly, as emotions you never knew you had begun to stir within you.

Why has this happened you ask yourself? Life can be so cruel!

Where has the calm and patient personality that trusts in God and his wonderful scriptures gone?

Will I ever make sense of all this?

Oh, how you wish this wasn't really happening. Moments of the loved one's mental clarity resurrect, and hope stirs within, only to be shattered quickly as symptoms rear their ugly head once more and those hopes are crashed.

Nothing seems plannable anymore. Shopping trips become a nightmare of hoping they will stay with you and not disappear up one of the shopping aisles, only to say when at last found "I was having a browse around!"

The nightmare rides in the car before assessment for the cessation of driving.

The accident that finally decides for them and the pain of watching them come to terms with it after many years of being on the road.

And so on and so forth – day in and day out. Torn between anguish and deep pain as you watch someone slowly disappearing in front of your eyes.

"When you finally accept that it's OK not to have answers and it's OK not to be perfect, you realize that feeling confused is a normal part of what it is to be a human being."

-Winona Ryder

3 *You are on your own!*

Everyone's journey will have different manifestations, but the inner turmoil of emotions is nevertheless much the same.

Sometimes it can seem a lonely journey, in spite of the support offered and where back-up help resides. Plus, we have to always bear in mind that they may not want intrusion because in their mind they do not want to be seen to be different.

This is where help that is offered has to be denied due to the development of the gradual ongoing non-compliance – understandable as they think they are perfectly OK!

One's own feelings of "I CAN do this" can be a stumbling block to gradually getting compliance or trying your best to, as the short-term memory will often times forget what had been agreed. E.g., one moment agreement for morning help and then the night before a major "sundowning" tirade of abuse and refusal.

No choice but to go it alone and keep your chin up and try to be calm and energized at all times.

What is also interesting is that the first person asked about is the patient who is mostly oblivious to what is going on and the carer forgotten. People of course mean well and are showing kindness so forgiven in the main.

Then of course, as I said earlier, maybe carers can be their own worst enemy as they put on the brave face and when maybe asked how they are coping "Oh, I'm fine" – must not be seen to not be coping while feeling isolated and alone inside.

> *"Loneliness and the feeling of being unwanted is the most terrible poverty."*
>
> ***-Mother Teresa***

I was communicating with a lovely lady "across the pond" and it became SO clear about how lonely the journey can be with a lack of empathetic and positive emotional support.

It is my belief that as human beings we have lost who we truly are – an expression of universal or God Consciousness and don't really know how to tap into that place of unconditional love and peace that is always there. It becomes covered up by all of our programming and experience responses. Never mind the way we are always encouraged to look outside ourselves for happiness and peace.

Our world seems to encourage feelings of fear and sadness rather than feelings of contentment and inner calm.

It is no wonder that on painful journeys there doesn't seem to be any answers and feelings of desperation and loneliness engulf. Mother Theresa is right with her quote. Feeling alone is like an inner poverty that leaves you almost unable to find a way out.

As well as focusing on the inevitable outcomes with this disease, it is essential to help carers find a way to deal with their emotions.

I can recall one particular time after numerous sleepless nights and being amazingly calm whilst witnessing the inner turmoil my loved one was going through, as one was "keep on keeping on" regardless, with challenging days and sleepless nights that left me in "shreds"! I am sure you may relate to this.

I found myself speaking to my husband in a such a way that I unconsciously "got it wrong". He said something to me that was a little harsh and I responded – as I thought – in my usual manner. However, the words came out of my mouth with a tinge of exasperation. His response was – "How dare you speak to me like that! I never speak to you like that!" Fortunately, I had learned much by now and apologised and told him that sometimes I got tired and my calmness seemed to disappear at that moment. Note that I did not play on the fact that he often "lost it".

Inevitably you are going to be irritable at times and lose your patience as you do your level best to remain in control.

When you are walking a tightrope every day it is going to be understandable that you will not get it right all the time. This will of course start emotional triggers of feeling bad about not getting it right every time.

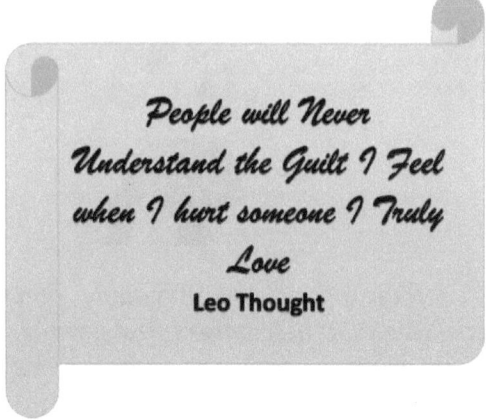

People will Never Understand the Guilt I Feel when I hurt someone I Truly Love
Leo Thought

Oh yes! That saying says it all! I recall a song from back in the 60's by *The Mills Brothers*. The first two lines are:

"You Always Hurt the One You Love

The One You Shouldn't Hurt at All"

Maybe the second line could read – "the one I don't want to hurt at all."

Sometimes you can be so deep in the pain of what is happening that even thinking about happy times can trigger sadness because they have now been lost in the mist of the carer journey. The sense of togetherness has disappeared from your life, and all seems terribly lost. Even in company there is a gaping wound inside that you fear will never heal.

4 Alighting the Roller Coaster

When you were a child, you may have gone to a fairground or a theme park. Here in the United Kingdom, we have two famous ones – Alton Towers and Chessington World of Adventures as well as the ones at seaside resorts e.g., Blackpool is famous for its fairground rides.

I was never a lover of fairgrounds and the rides. I remember, after much persuasion, going on a roller coaster and wanting to jump off without a single thought of how far down it was to the ground. The up and down and round and round journey only filled me with inner terror and panic.

I even know some real "macho" men who also hate the rides.

Fear is no respecter of persons and can be triggered in a moment over all sorts of things.

So, where is this leading to?

If you think about the journey as a carer, it very much resembles a ride on a roller coaster.

Riding the Emotional Roller Coaster: *The Emotional Journey of Caring*

You get on the ride thinking you will do the ride just fine! – "I can handle this!"

Then – Oh My! The ride begins and it turns out to be for many, not an exciting ride but one of absolute terror and you want to stop it, but you can't.

You are probably OK on the upward bit of the ride but then - all seems to take a rushed downward turn and fast circles that you cannot control, just trying to deal with your fear.

It seems to go on forever and when you can get off you don't feel too great either and hide the inner feelings of nausea and panic as you are not going to allow others to see how scared you are.

For me that roller coaster ride truly illustrates the journey of a Carer, only in this case it is like you were thrust on the ride without much warning and maybe in some moments wish you could run from it all but somehow you know there is no turning back and even don't really want to run, just be able to take the ride more calmly.

Right now, I am trying to be in a place of calm, a place where I can chill out and then handle the chaos of life better. You don't just get it overnight; you have to work at it. It's a daily struggle.

-Jackee Harry

5 *Is There a Stop to this Ride?*

If you think about a fairground roller coaster ride that you go on with fear and trepidation, once you are on it you feel as if you are never going to get off. A few minutes seems like a lifetime!

However, eventually the up and down and round and round ride of terror comes to an end. You may well be brave enough to have future rides and be determined to overcome the fear and talk yourself into being calm throughout the whole ride.

This of course doesn't happen immediately but with time and consistent work on your reactions you eventually realise that you can do the ride because you have created inner calm about the up and down and round and round of this almighty roller coaster.

Once mastered, any roller coaster ride then becomes something you cope with without abject fear. You are then assuring others that the ride is not that difficult to do and that if you mastered it, so can they.

Imagine this being the case with the journey as a carer. It all seems so daunting and the possibility of finding inner calm a definite no-no.

People around are keen to help you but cannot deal with the inner self that you are living with from day-to-day, moment by moment.

Let's go back to the fairground ride again. Friends re-assure you that it will be fine and that everyone gets terrified but turn it into something that is fun and exciting. You think that they must be joking! Find fun and humour in something that terrifies you? Impossible!

They of course are Not You! They are on their own ride.

Then maybe someone talks about breathing strategies and imagining the ride as something else that is not scary and you decide to try it. With practice it works and you feel a sense of achievement that you have overcome the fear you once had and can handle any ride with the strategy offered.

You may, in amongst everything associated with this emotional roller coaster, also wonder why you have inner panics, fear about the future of the carer journey. Why these emotions seem to rule your life from day to day.

Where do they come from?

I've never had these feelings before.

Not that I can readily recall, you think to yourself.

We will consider this in the following chapters as we identify some of the key emotions associated with your roller coaster ride.

For now, accept that life is really like a roller coaster ride of experiences and being a carer is another experience that has come your way. It can seem a bit terrifying when it is suddenly thrust upon you without warning.

Sometimes The Hardest Thing And The Right Thing Are the Same

It is true that sometimes in life we know that we must make a certain decision and that it will be tough going but the thing to do, is, having made the choice to find strategies that will ease the way and turn the experience into something really amazing that empowers you and brings out the very best in you.

> *The truth is you don't know what is going to happen tomorrow. Life is a crazy ride, and nothing is guaranteed.*
>
> *-Eminem*

So, if you chose the ride as a carer or if it was thrust upon you then you might as well make a decision to find a way of dealing with it and find the way to control your ride.

That seems somewhat patronizing, doesn't it?

What helped me on my own roller coaster ride of caring with my husband's Young Onset Alzheimer's Disease was to seek out a strategy that would assist in finding the deep inner calm within my spirit.

I call it,

"The 3 A's of the Caring Journey"

1. A - for **Acknowledge** what is taking place

2. A – for **Adjust** the way you handle the situation

3. A – for **Accept** that you handle this day/moment only and use the **"3 A's"** for the next day or moment that changes that may need a whole different approach

6 The Secret to Finding the Stop Button

"You have power over your mind—not outside events. Realize this, and you will find strength."

-Marcus Aurelius - 121-180 AD
Roman Emperor

When you are going through emotionally charged life experiences, it is easy to get caught up in the drama of it all.

We are essentially programmed beings from birth and go through life responding to situations from our programming. This means that you may well react to current things happening in your life from a perspective that relates to a trigger mechanism many years back.

Your brain is but a switching station and stores memories as well as keeping your amazing body systems functioning. For example, as I type this script, my mind is transferring thought messages to the brain and signals are passed through the nervous system to my fingers and triggers are sent back to the brain which fires more signals to the correct muscles so that I will type the words down with my fingers. As well as the signals to my visual cortex in the brain so that I observe the correct keys to press. Never mind memory triggers for the correct spelling of the words!!

The Brain is made up of trillions of neurons that fire off signals according to information received from the outside environment.

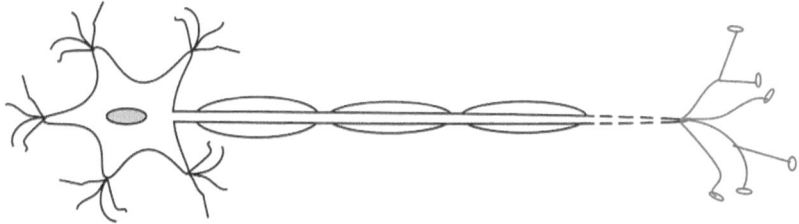

This is an illustration of a typical neuron in your Brain.

Therefore, if you have laid down certain memories from your childhood that are associated with certain triggers that occurred, producing specific emotional responses, those same triggers will occur later in life.

Science has discovered incredible things about our brains and how those neurons of yours work together. They can either fire signals that are empowering and positive or disempowering and negative depending on the information you feed it.

It is this programmed mind that causes triggers to the neurons, that the key to getting off the emotional roller coaster lies.

So here you are on your emotional roller coaster.

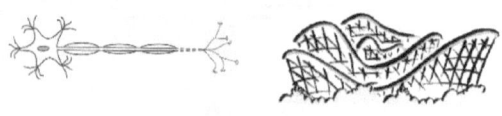

Your Brain has Trillions of these neurons.

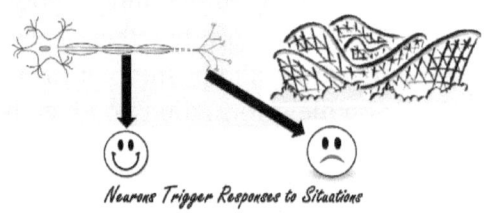

These neurons trigger different responses.

Depending on your past programming you will have a different type of response

OR

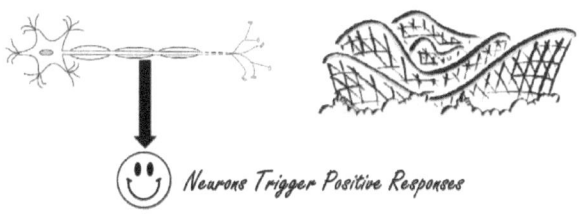

The thing to recognize here is that on this roller coaster journey, the emotions you are experiencing will be rooted in past programmed responses to fearful and uncertain situations as well as responses triggered from verbal input from other people around you that made you feel alienated or not part of the group.

A mindset programmed to negative emotional responses can be changed with dedicated and persistent commitment.

Now – suppose you could do some simple mind techniques and respond differently to the situations that trigger guilt, denial, anger or grief?

Yes, indeed! The key to getting off the emotional roller coaster is to work with the mind and re-program responses so that you cope with your journey differently and positively.

The next step is to consider these four key emotions in more detail and the way in which you can find a positive solution.

7 Letting Go of the Guilt

What you believe is very powerful. If you have toxic emotions of fear, guilt and depression, it is because you have wrong thinking, and you have wrong thinking because of wrong believing.

-Joseph Prince

You grow up programmed to believe that you always have to "tow the party line" rather than follow your own intuition.

If you deviate from what is collectively believed to be the norm you are made to feel uncomfortable by your peers.

From a tiny infant in many ways, you are on a guilt trip as you stifle creativity and "do as you are told". Threats of punishment are all part of daily routine.

Now, of course, children growing up need to know that in life there are certain unavoidable boundaries.

However, it is how these are communicated that decides whether they grow up empowered to make choices and respond in positive ways to challenges or whether they become victims to circumstances.

All the "stuff" that enters the head of a child from aged 0 – 7 years of age lays the foundation for their values and beliefs about life. For example - how often have you, if you are a parent said, "I will never say that to my child!". Then the very day comes some years later and out of your mouth come almost the self-same words you heard when you were growing up. That is what programming is all about.

My own life was programmed around guilt big time - "Hurry up and get your homework done, it's the prayer meeting at eight o'clock!". I then would feel double guilt, one about not being ready for church plus what I would tell teacher for unfinished homework!

That and many other things meant that I went into adulthood ready to feel guilty at a moment's notice about anything. Until of course I did something about the past programming.

Can you recall moments way back in your life where you were sent on a real big guilt trip?

Now here's the thing. That experience left a memory code deep in your subconscious mind and neuron trigger mechanisms. Any future situations that are centered around the potential to feel guilt fire off the same triggers and the guilt mechanism kicks in automatically. That means that the guilt that you feel on this journey about how you should be coping is not valid. You can release the feelings and look at the situation from the point of view that you are doing the very best with what you have and where you are right now.

On my journey as a carer, I had many moments where I would beat myself up and feel guilty because "I could do it better!". Where did all that come from? One day it dawned on me – yes, the school reports *"tries hard but could do better!"* was just one of the many experiences.

In any event in your life, you can only do what you can do in that moment with what you have to the best of your ability. You won't get it right all the time – I am still learning and then passing my learnings on to others. You can do that too!

The sooner you deal with guilt you will feel empowered to accept that you are doing the best you can and that it is nobody else's business to tell you otherwise but maybe in love share how they have learned to deal with their own guilt.

Do this exercise: -

- Write down in detail a past experience where you went on a major guilt trip over something. Really get into the whole scenario – where it happened, who was in the setting, the conversation, how you responded and the emotions you felt. Be creative with it and if tears come that is great because you are releasing emotions that have been buried deep. Write from your heart without thought or judgement.

- Now tear the paper into tiny pieces as you say this mantra, out loud with feeling:

"I NOW STEP INTO THE POWER OF KNOWING THAT I AM ALWAYS DOING THE VERY BEST I CAN IN ALL CIRCUMSTANCES OF MY LIFE!"

- Finally, either burn the paper or bury it in the garden to rot while you continue to recite the mantra.

Congratulate yourself and celebrate a new you with a ritual that reinforces your release technique.

Every day before rising say the following five times with feeling:

TODAY AND EVERY DAY I AM LIVING IN PEACE AND POWER.
I DO EVERYTHING TO THE VERY BEST OF MY ABILITY

If you are a follower of Jesus, remember this scripture –

Trust in the LORD with all your heart and lean not on your own understanding; in all your ways submit to him, and He will make your paths straight.

-Proverbs Ch. 3 verses 5, 6

8 *Making Denial a Positive Tool*

My first thought as I consider denial is from my childhood days of being taught the Holy Bible inside/out and the story of the crucifixion of Jesus where the disciple Peter denied knowing Jesus three times after saying he never would. Denial is a part of the spectrum of emotional responses to what is going on in your life. The important thing is to be aware as to why you are in denial and if it is being used positively or not.

Here's a quote that illustrates what we are about to get into:

> *It's not denial.*
> *I'm just selective about*
> *the reality I accept.*
>
> *-Bill Watterson*

On the carers journey, I believe there are two components to denial which links well with the above quote.

Let's consider the first use of denial which is a common affliction when you live in fear and want to run away from challenges instead of facing them head on.

I recall a situation way back in my life where because I was still living a fear and worry based life, I had been unfairly accused of things at work. I had to write a statement. In the first interview I allowed senior management to basically get me confused and answering questions in a way that almost made me guilty. I had to write a statement which would have been 100% the truth and ended the whole scenario but I procrastinated and went into fear of consequences and basically tried to pretend the experience wasn't happening until my counsellor gave me a deadline and I faced up to things square in the eye and did what I had to do.

When challenges come to you in life it is so easy to become like the ostrich.

Put your head in the sand and totally ignore what is going on.

I learned a great lesson from my denial tactic and from then on vowed I would NEVER be like the Ostrich EVER again.

Life is always going to throw some stuff at you to see how well you will deal with it and you cannot go through your life pretending things aren't happening.

"Oh! Tomorrow it will all be better."

"No! they didn't really say that did they?"

"No! I am imagining their behavior – it is just a passing phase!"

Doing this with Alzheimer's or any other situation you are about to become a carer with, will neither benefit You or the Person who needs to be diagnosed and helped. What will happen is that one day something will occur that smacks you right in the eye and denial is not an option! A crisis occurs which, if you had taken your head out of the sand and faced things head on, even in the face of the challenge of diplomatically communicating with the person needing to be medically diagnosed, would create different results.

You see, I used to literally pray for the right time to face my dear man with "Darling, I don't know how to put this but something seems to be not quite right………We need to get you to a Doctor" Then one day it was as if somebody just took over my mouth and over a cup of tea I managed to say what needed to be said. What happened next was truly amazing. His response was "Funny you should say that darling. You know I have noticed for a while now that, for example, when I make a cup of coffee it doesn't seem to go right, and the water misses the cup." I could then get compliance about going to the doctor.

Yes, it is painful, learning to accept You are in denial as well as the person with Alzheimer's. The thing is this, that at some point it has to be faced, and the sooner the better, to facilitate as positive a strategy as possible on the journey one faces.

A tough one to accept maybe but here is a quote from the wonderful Reverend Michael Bernard Beckwith of the Agape Spiritual Centre in California –

It Is What Is, accept it – Harvest The Good – Forgive All The Rest

Again, your denial response may be linked to a prior situation that needs acknowledging and releasing.

Repeat the exercise you did around Guilt, but this time write about a situation or situations that you know you were in denial about – let it all just flow out on to the paper and follow through with the ritual but using this mantra—

I FACE ALL CHALLENGES IN MY LIFE HEAD ON

I KNOW THE SOLUTIONS ARE COMING TO ME NOW

Repeat this mantra five times each morning also. Neuroscience shows that repetition re-programs the unconscious mind. With 30-60 days' discipline it works. By then you will have remembered them and can use them throughout the day as well.

So, how do we use the emotion of denial in a positive way?

I recall listening to the local radio station a few years back soon after my husband had been diagnosed with his Young Onset Alzheimer's Disease. The presenter was talking with a lady who was on the journey with her husband. She was asked if she had any advice for others. "My advice is to carry on life as if they haven't got Alzheimer's."

"A great tip" I thought to myself and began living it every day. It seemed to work well UNTIL one fateful day I got caught out. Now pretty much fully playing the whole denial game I was not prepared for a day of sudden extreme verbal abuse and 100% non-compliance with anything!!

Once again, I was on a learning curve and figured out a new game of balanced denial.

What do I mean by that? You live each day *as if all is as it was* BUT you are ready also to jump into carer patience and inner calm with their behavior. Recognizing the warning signs that usually show in the eyes and a change in facial expression which means you keep your distance and use tactics that prevent a major drama.

When you can create this daily pattern of coping, you and the person diagnosed are calmer and YOU deal with sudden changes much more calmly and positively.

I had my own mantra I used when we were still dealing with things at home – feel free to adopt it as I give to carers that take advantage of the Dementia Whisper Carer Support tools.

As you take a deep breath in and sigh it out say to yourself "**I CHOOSE PEACE – ALL IS WELL IN MY WORLD.**"

With practice like the other mantras, it will work. Many a day whilst at the kitchen sink, I would repeat the mantra quietly and was able to de-stress.

So, say goodbye to and welcome in: -

Balance and

9 Dealing with Frustration and Anger

For every minute you remain angry, you give up sixty seconds of peace of mind.

-Ralph Waldo Emerson

Ralph Waldo Emerson is renowned for some very wise sayings, not least the one above.

What do we mean by anger?

Here is what *Collins Dictionary* defines anger as: **Anger-** a feeling of great annoyance or antagonism as the result of some real or supposed grievance; rage; wrath.

Anger is one of a whole spectrum of emotions that definitely needs handling positively. Suppressed anger is one of the major causes of disease in the body manifesting such conditions as cancer and chronic illnesses, as the energy of unexpressed feelings are more and more suppressed resulting in an energetic imbalance within the cells and body systems. A healthy body is one that has minimum stress and knows how to handle it in a way that is beneficial to overall wellbeing.

If we could teach anger management techniques to all humanity, I believe we would end all strife and dissensions on our beautiful planet.

Part of being a carer is handling all sorts of emotions that are fired at you and then dealing with your own response emotions, anger being one of them.

I was brought up to be a quiet conforming child and therefore grew up having to learn how to express my own feelings and emotions. Programmed with fear-based identity, I suppressed true feelings and became the classic "doormat". Mustn't get angry! I since learned that All emotions need expression for a balanced and healthy being to be lived out.

So, the message here is that anger must be:

Acknowledged – expressed – controlled

Let us now take a look at those threes in action -

Owning up to the fact that we are feeling angry is the first positive step towards healing anger issues.

You are going to have moments of anger and frustration as you watch someone you love visibly changing in front of you. It is a perfectly natural response and must be accepted by you that it is now a part of you that needs attention, especially if you are a person who has never been really angry over things in life.

When anger is suddenly released as an outburst the brain neurons fire signals that increases the heart rate and sets up tension in the blood vessels – you run the greater risk of a heart attack or stroke. Controlled expression of anger will be of greater benefit to your health.

I recall when anger and frustration reared their ugly head on my journey with Brian. It seemed so unnatural to me. I could count on less than one hand how many times I had got acutely wound up. One such incident was in my nursing days when I was in charge of a ward while the sister in charge took forced sick leave for "women's" surgery and was away for at least three months.

It was a typical day on the ward and for the umpteenth time I had asked a junior nurse to ensure a certain important task was completed during the shift. It seemed to fall on incredibly deaf ears and I "lost it" big time! With absolute rage I shouted at her in the middle of the ward and all the other staff plus the patients went quiet. You could have heard a pin drop! It gave the desired result, but I realized I should have handled it differently and had the grace to speak to her in the office as well as apologizing not only to her but everyone else. The patients thought it quite amusing! Probably the best entertainment for a while for them! Maybe I was also projecting suppressed anger through that situation as well.

So, if you find yourself having angry frustrated feelings on this journey it would be a great idea to take a look back at past situations like the two previous exercises and seek to release it on paper – by now you may be filling up an A4 pad!!

For this one, the mantra to work with has been mentioned already. Again, repeat five times in the morning on rising but use frequently throughout the day if you need to, whilst taking in that deep breath and sighing out all the frustrations and anger of the moment—

I CHOOSE PEACE IN THIS SITUATION

ALL IS WELL

I love the quote below. It is the best anger management advice for me. While you are in anger mode, use the mantra above.

"The greatest remedy for anger is delay."

-Thomas Paine

10 Getting to Grips with Grief

"I remember my aunt telling me however I chose to handle this would be the right way. There isn't a handbook or a script. You just take it as it comes, One day at a time

I love the quote that opens this chapter. It is perfect for anyone on the caring journey.

You cannot make predictions about how the journey will pan out. On this journey, you are grieving day to day in some way the dying of someone before they eventually leave the physical form.

I recall in the early days of our Alzheimer's journey responding to Brian's frustrations with "It's those Naughty Neurons again!" This then became the phrase used to help cope with the changes manifesting as more and more neuron activity changed and died. It helped greatly, and in the early days, we ended up laughing every day about the naughty neurons. The real Brian existed somewhere. His spirit would not ever die, and our love would go on forever.

For the carer the day-to-day grieving can be hard and the grief will manifest through the other emotions we have discussed.

I cannot stress strongly enough the importance of expressing your grief so that it doesn't suddenly overwhelm you and lead to depression. Regular small bursts of release keep everything in perspective and help you carry on.

It is SO important to know that on the Alzheimer's journey you are not seeing the real person reacting to and responding to their environment. Yes, in the moment of the "out of character" behavior you may well instinctively respond as you would have done before. Don't get angry with them or yourself. It is what is in that moment.

So how do we deal with the grief that bubbles up?

Let me share one of my moments with you. I visited Brian in the Princess Christian Care Home where he resided, and he was on a bad day – hadn't had a really bad one for a while - and in angry mood about everything. I was stupid and didn't know what I was talking about as I tried desperately to understand what he was endeavoring to communicate. Nothing would divert him and eventually I was told to f... off out of it. And so, I did, as I was on a losing wicket. Having been caught off guard, I went into grieving mode as I drove home with tears streaming down my face. Having created strategies for coping by now, when I got indoors, I took me in hand and coached me!

On went the kettle to make a cup of tea and then I sat at the dining table, tea to one side and closed my eyes. I allowed more tears to flow for a couple of minutes and then mentally visualized our beautiful wedding day, re-living every moment as if it was happening right then. Within a few minutes I was at peace and knew that what I had been through earlier was not my man but his jumbled neurons firing off. I frequently think of the good times, happy memories and will laugh to myself and give thanks for his love and the joy he brought into my life.

The key to dealing with your grief is to remind yourself that somewhere there is a memory of a typical happy time that will lift you up mentally and get into that whole scenario and fully relive it as if it is happening Right Now! Keep practicing it and you will become an expert at it.

Carers, you need to look after your own physical health. Your nervous and immune systems can be drained as you continue this roller coaster ride.

Look after you and you are better able to care for others.

Another scripture from the Bible is–

Love Thy Neighbour AS Thyself, the Master Jesus taught.

I recall having the first part drummed into me when truly the last phrase is the most important. How can you help others if we don't first love yourself?

Then be open to let others help you and nurture you from time to time. Let go and let quality carers step in and help. It is so easy to become a martyr to the cause and let good old guilt come in.

When my dear man first went into full time care into what can only be described as a five-star care home, I still brought his washing home and rushed in every day to visit him. Then one day the head nurse called me into the office "Sylvia, you are tired, I can see it in your eyes. Brian is being cared for. He is safe and if anything occurs, we will call you". I made a promise to stay away for five days. I kid you not, it was as if my soul had been ripped out, but I did it. Guess what? He was fine and had lost time memory and we had a great visit together. That was another learning curve and gradually I set a routine of visiting days with Sunday Roast Lunch a must! We had more and more quality visits and I adjusted to the not so good days.

Take Care of You!!
Grieve Positively
Cherish the Great Happy Memories!!

11 *Turning Learnings Into Service*

There is nothing more fulfilling than turning your own experiences and learnings into a gift to help others.

That I vowed to do with my husband in the early days of our Alzheimer's journey.

First came the book about the ups and downs of our journey including major challenges around getting married but also with tips and learnings along the way.

Writing our story and sharing what I learned has been a very rewarding project and I am blessed that it is helping others since its original publication in 2016.

Even getting the first book published was what I would call Divine synchronicity. It was only publisher number three that I contacted who when I called responded with "My father had dementia. This sounds really interesting. Please send me the transcript!" Within three days the contract was signed. I bless my lovely man for agreeing to help others through this journey. Now re-published all books are available at: -

https://dementia-whisperer.com/publications

This book has given you some guidance around dealing with the emotional roller coaster ride. What the key emotions are and how you can use strategies for coping.

I am sure with practice every day you will feel more in control of how you continue your caring role.

It took me disciplined practice to achieve full results and be able to be at peace and not have big butterflies of agitation when visiting Brian.

I still used the naughty neurons phrase as a coping mechanism and would say to myself whilst driving to see him – "I wonder how Mr. Naughty Neurons will be today?" What a joy it was to drive down Stafford Lake in Knaphill in Surrey and approach Princess Christian Care Home free of emotional knots and nausea in my Solar Plexus!

Remember consistent work on changing how you do the caring journey will bring results. The important thing is *to keep on keeping on* until you succeed.

THAT'S WHAT I DID AND WHY I SHARE IT WITH YOU NOW.

> **Strength does not come from winning. Your struggles develop your strengths. When you go through hardships and decide not to surrender, that is strength**
> Mahatma Ghandi

There is opportunity to delve deeper into these emotions and impact on all areas of your life. Learn more about your programmed mind and how to re-programme those messed up neurons.

Inspired one weekend, brought about the development of Dementia Whisperer.

The best emotional support actually lies deep within all of us. You will be a better carer if you can develop the "inner skills" and tap into the real authentic you that God created and desired that you find Inner Calm in troubled times.

From the Bible, Jesus speaks -

> *Peace, I leave with you, My peace I give to you; not as the world gives do I give to you. Let not your heart be troubled, neither let it be afraid.*
>
> ***-John 14 v 27***

To find out more about Dementia Whisperer and the support services Sylvia offers take a visit to –

https://dementia-whisperer.com

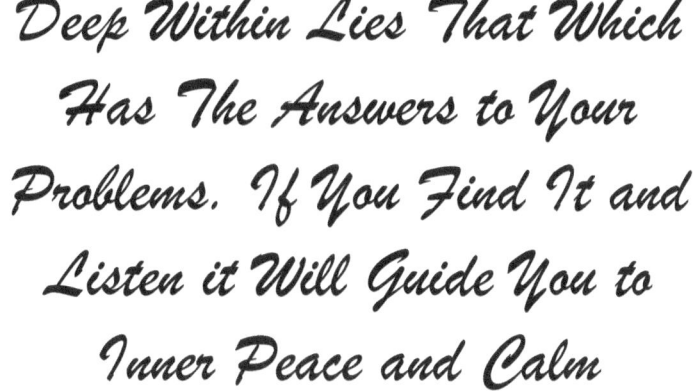

Deep Within Lies That Which Has The Answers to Your Problems. If You Find It and Listen it Will Guide You to Inner Peace and Calm

About the Author

Sylvia, whose mother told her she was born looking like a "skinned rabbit", overcame a sickly childhood to achieve a successful nursing career including Nurse Counselling, Community Care and Managing a Care Home.

She also was brought up to know that God can be our comfort in troubling times.

Casting all your care upon Him; for He careth for you.

-1Peter Ch.5 v 7

Fun and success in the medical sales and marketing arena was a step out of her comfort zone and another challenge faced head on.

Overcoming her own health issues led to researching the alternative health arena and subsequently training to become an Accredited Master Coach.

Becoming a carer with her husband on the Young Onset Alzheimer's Journey was to really test her knowledge, skills, and Christian faith, which subsequently led to a calling to develop emotional support tools to help other carers experiencing emotional challenge.

Go to - https://dementia-whisperer.com

For more information about her Emotional Support Services and read about how she achieved Inner Peace throughout her own journey

www.ingramcontent.com/pod-product-compliance
Lightning Source LLC
LaVergne TN
LVHW040202080526
838202LV00042B/3284